SOUSA'S GREAT MARCHES

IN PIANO TRANSCRIPTION

SOUSA'S GREAT MARCHES

IN PIANO TRANSCRIPTION

Original Sheet Music of 23 Works by

JOHN PHILIP SOUSA

Selected, with an introduction, by
LESTER S. LEVY

Dover Publications, Inc., New York

Sousa's Great Marches in Piano Transcription is a new work, first
published by Dover Publications, Inc., in 1975.

The publisher is grateful to Mr. Lester S. Levy for making the
original sheet music in his collection available for reproduction.

International Standard Book Number: 0-486-23132-1
Library of Congress Catalog Card Number: 73-93543

Manufactured in the United States of America
Dover Publications, Inc.
180 Varick Street
New York, N Y. 10014

Introduction

Throughout the years, particular musical groups, or occasionally individual performers, have captured the hearts of the American public. Our present youth, who most recently have related to the newer varieties of sound produced by combinations like the Allman Brothers, the Grateful Dead and the Beach Boys, were only a short while back shouting at the bland ballads of the Beatles or swooning over the gyrations of Elvis Presley. Their parents were willing to travel many miles for the privilege of listening to, and dancing to, the strains of bands under the leadership of Benny Goodman and Paul Whiteman.

But for the men and women and children of the turn-of-the-century era there was one name only that had universal appeal in the field of music—John Philip Sousa. Sousa was a cult—a joyous cult.

From 1880—when, at the age of 26, he was appointed leader of the United States Marine Band—to 1919, when he left the United States Navy at the end of World War I, he was the symbol of all that was thrilling in American music. Between his devotion to these two government services, there was a long and honorable career as bandmaster to the American public and as composer of some of the most stirring music ever written.

Sousa's father was of Portuguese ancestry; his mother was German; but there was nothing old-worldly about either their son or his melodic genius. Born in Washington, in 1854, he started to master the violin at the age of seven, and in six years had progressed to the point where he was offered a position with a band attached to a circus. Sousa's father circumvented this dubious form of employment by arranging to enlist him in the Marine Band as an apprentice.

Five years with the Marines was enough for the would-be conductor. He managed to withdraw from its band, and within months was leading a small traveling orchestra and indulging in his first attempts at composition. At twenty, he was finding music publishers willing to accept his material, which, at the outset, consisted of songs and miscellaneous pieces, with an occasional attempt at light opera. The marches—the works which would win him a permanent place in American musical history—came a bit later on.

Once again the Marine Band lured him back into government service—this time as bandmaster, a position which he filled under five presidents. It was during this period, when Sousa's band was performing at the most important government functions, that the earliest of his great marches were presented to the public.

Introduction

His first real hit came in 1886. It was "The Gladiator," a march which was to set the style for the many successful works to follow. From coast to coast, bands included it in their repertoire; at one big parade in Philadelphia, seventeen marching bands were heard playing "The Gladiator."

Within the next few years, while Sousa was still in his early thirties, he turned out many of his greatest marches—"Semper Fidelis," the stirring march adopted by the Marine Corps; "The High School Cadets"; "The Washington Post."

A march dedicated to a newspaper was a fanciful idea, and it came about because of the newspaper's interest in encouraging literary expression in the public schools. In 1889 the *Post* staged a contest and offered prizes for the best essays written by pupils, and it arranged to award the prizes on the grounds of the Smithsonian Institution, where the participants and visitors were to be entertained with musical selections by the Marine Band. Several days before the event, one of the proprietors of the *Post* asked Sousa to write a march in celebration of the contest. Sousa was delighted to oblige. "The Washington Post March," performed for the first time on June 15, 1889, before twenty thousand children and their parents and friends, proved to be one of the half dozen greatest that Sousa ever wrote.

At this time the dancing masters of the country were endeavoring to introduce a new ballroom dance which they called the "two-step," and they agreed that "The Washington Post" was the tune which would insure the new dance's popularity. The success of the two-step was assured forthwith; on the ballroom floor the waltz was soon relegated to second place.

Like another famous American composer, Stephen Foster, young Sousa was no businessman when it came to disposing of his wares. Some of his finest early marches were sold to Harry Coleman, a shrewd Philadelphia publisher, for thirty-five dollars apiece. The enormous profits which resulted brought Sousa not an extra penny, but enabled Coleman to build reed and brass instrument factories from the proceeds of the distribution of Sousa marches.

As leader of the Marine Band, Sousa was hardly in the front rank of well-to-do Americans. His salary was in the neighborhood of $1500 a year. Small wonder that when he was offered a fourfold increase in salary and a profit-sharing arrangement if he would conduct a band of his own, he was unable to resist; and for the second time in his life he decided to sever his connection with the United States government. So, in 1892, Sousa's resignation as leader of the Marine Band was accepted with regret, and he set about organizing his own great band. His prestige attracted the finest individual performers among the country's brass and woodwind instrumentalists. The band was a leading attraction at the Chicago World's Fair in 1893. During that same year it enjoyed the unusual distinction of performing with Walter Damrosch and the New York Philharmonic Symphony in Carnegie Hall.

And now Sousa began to realize that his compositions had enormous potential value. The year after the birth of his new band, he signed a contract with the publisher John Church of Cincinnati in which he was guaranteed the usual royalties to which a composer is entitled. One of the first marches composed after this arrangement had been entered into was "The Liberty Bell," which within a few years netted Sousa $35,000. On other later marches his income was many times that amount.

The greatest of all Sousa's marches was conceived late in 1896 as he was on a homeward trip after a European vacation. As Sousa paced the deck (he wrote in his autobiography, *Marching Along*) he "began to sense the rhythmic beat of a band playing within my brain. . . . Throughout the . . . voyage, that imaginary band continued to unfold the same themes, echoing and re-echoing the most distinct melody. I did not transfer a note of that music to paper while I was on the steamer, but when we reached shore I set down the measures that my brain-band had been playing for me,"

The composition born to Sousa on shipboard was "The Stars and Stripes Forever," probably the greatest and most widely performed popular march ever written. No important parade today would be complete without a rendition of this exciting work.

Back and forth across the country went Sousa and his trombonists, bassoonists, French-horn players, trumpeters, clarinetists, tuba players, saxophonists, oboists, cornetists and drummers. The largest horn was a helicon tuba which wound around a musician's body, with a huge bell which violently blared the music ahead of other instrumentalists. Sousa disliked this sound effect, and designed a giant horn with an upright bell, which diffused the tone to his satisfaction. The new instrument was given the name "Sousaphone" by its manufacturer, the Wurlitzer Company, and it is still an integral part of a brass band.

Sousa was not satisfied to confine his concerts to the United States. The band toured Europe four times, and in 1911 they took an ambitious trip around the world, bringing the great marches to South Africa and Australia, to New Zealand and the Fiji Islands and Hawaii, where, Sousa relates, he was decked with so many leis that his ears were hidden.

Sousa's friends and admirers included people famous in many fields. They ranged from Bob Fitzsimmons and John L. Sullivan, the prizefighters, to Admiral George Dewey, the hero of the Spanish-American War, to King Edward the Seventh of England, to Thomas A. Edison. When Leopold Stokowski, who later would become maestro of the Philadelphia Orchestra, first arrived in the United States, he attended a concert of Sousa's at New York's Hippodrome. Later, Stokowski said that the music swept him off his feet. The rhythm of Sousa stirred him; he recognized it as unique. From that time on, said Stokowski, he always wanted to meet "that musician with a pirate's beard."

The beard was an important part of Sousa's physiognomy until he joined the Navy upon America's entrance into World War I in 1917. A short stocky man, his appearance might have been undistinguished had it not been for the trim spade beard which, appearing above the high collar of the Marine dress uniform, seemed to enhance his martial image. During the twenty-five-year period when the band was Sousa's own, and not the Marines' or the Navy's, the beard was, in a way, Sousa's personal trademark. Always neat, with never a

Introduction

hair out of place, it was of a piece with his music, meticulous, flawless, clean-cut. Yet he removed it without a moment's hesitation soon after he joined the Navy. If it had been something of an affectation throughout the years, it had no place during wartime. From 1917 on, the trim gray moustache sufficed to complement Sousa's dignified bearing and polished showmanship.

To select examples of Sousa's finest marches for inclusion in this volume has been difficult. Every Sousa march has a unique personality, and every Sousa fan has his own favorites from among the more than one hundred marches that Sousa composed during his lifetime. "The Stars and Stripes Forever" will be at the top of most lists, and close behind will come "Semper Fidelis" and "The Washington Post" and the "Manhattan Beach" and "The High School Cadets" and "El Capitan," the unforgettable melody from his light opera of the same name.

The other seventeen reproduced represent those which have particular appeal for the author. A good piano sight-reader will find the arrangements easy to master, and the melodies and harmonies should bring back some of the emotions which stirred our grandparents three quarters of a century ago when they listened to the strains of the greatest band ever.

So, a-one, a-two . . .

LESTER S. LEVY

Baltimore, Md.

Contents

[The marches are arranged in chronological order.]

Contents

Alphabetical List
of Marches by Title

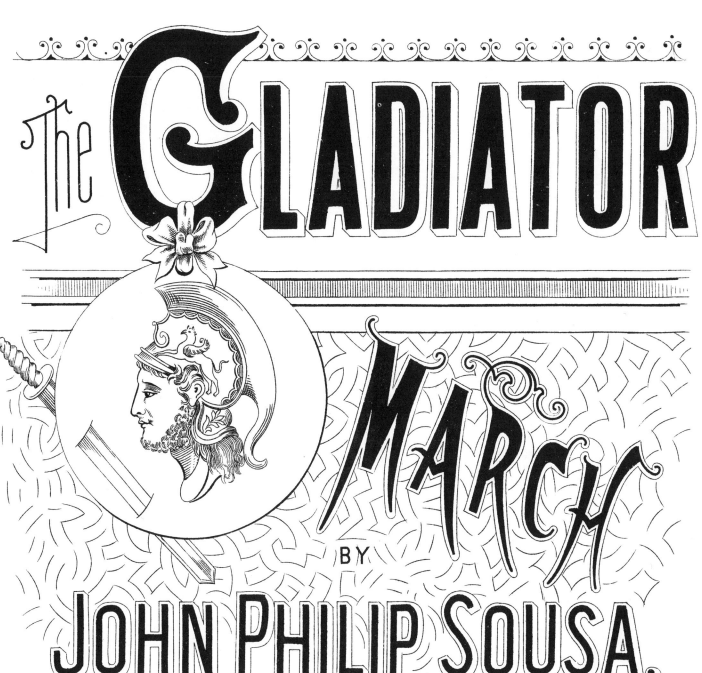

TO
Charles F. Towle.
BOSTON.

The GLADIATOR

MARCH

BY

JOHN PHILIP SOUSA.

DIRECTOR OF U.S. MARINE BAND.

FULL ORCHESTRA $1.00.
BAND. 50¢

Thorburn, N.Y.

SMALL ORCHESTRA. 60¢
PIANO. 40¢
FOR ONE OR TWO BANJO'S 30¢

PHILADELPHIA;
PUBLISHED BY HARRY COLEMAN,
PUBLISHER OF BAND AND ORCHESTRA MUSIC,
NO. 228 NORTH 9TH ST.

MARCH: THE GLADIATOR.

JOHN PHILIP SOUSA.

Trio.

The Gladiator   3

Grandioso.

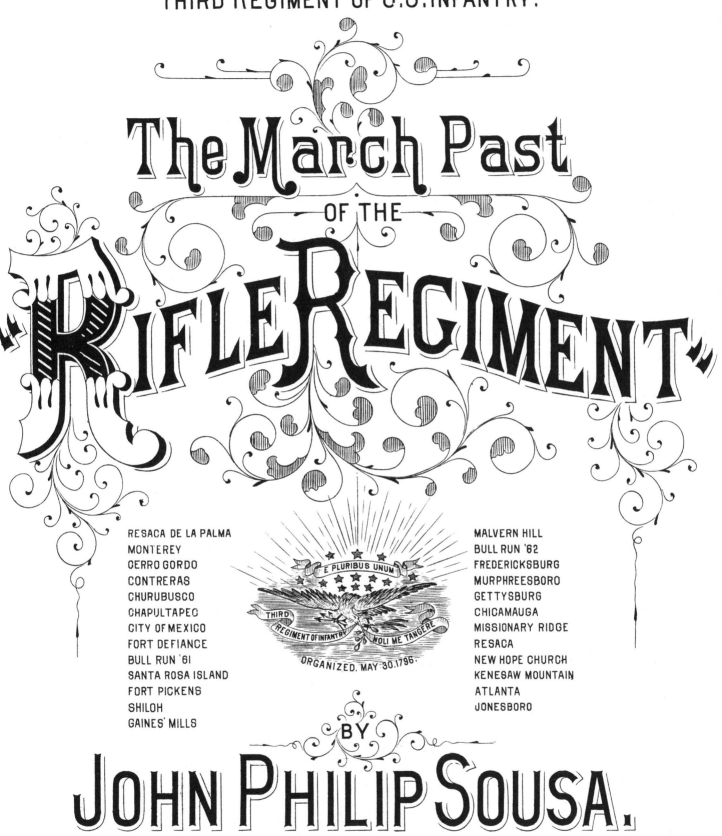

18th Edition.

To the Officers and Men of the
Third Regiment of U.S. Infantry.

The March Past

of the

Rifle Regiment

RESACA DE LA PALMA
MONTEREY
CERRO GORDO
CONTRERAS
CHURUBUSCO
CHAPULTAPEC
CITY OF MEXICO
FORT DEFIANCE
BULL RUN '61
SANTA ROSA ISLAND
FORT PICKENS
SHILOH
GAINES' MILLS

E PLURIBUS UNUM
THIRD REGIMENT OF INFANTRY
NOLI ME TANGERE
ORGANIZED, MAY 30, 1796.

MALVERN HILL
BULL RUN '62
FREDERICKSBURG
MURPHREESBORO
GETTYSBURG
CHICAMAUGA
MISSIONARY RIDGE
RESACA
NEW HOPE CHURCH
KENESAW MOUNTAIN
ATLANTA
JONESBORO

BY

John Philip Sousa.

DIRECTOR OF MARINE BAND.

Piano, 50
Orch.ª 60. 80. 1.00
Mil. Band, 50

Mandolin 30 with Piano or Guitar 40.
2 Mandolins 40 " " " 50.
Banjo Solo or Duet 30 " " " 40.
Guitar Solo 30 " " or 2d Guitar 40.

NEW YORK,

PUBLISHED BY CARL FISCHER, 6 FOURTH AVE.

THE RIFLE-REGIMENT MARCH.

John Philip Sousa.

TRIO.

To the
OFFICERS AND MEN
OF THE
UNITED STATES MARINE CORPS.

Semper Fidelis MARCH

BY

JOHN PHILIP SOUSA.

BAND MASTER UNITED STATES MARINE CORPS.

Solo. Duet.

6

CARL FISCHER,
COOPER SQUARE, NEW YORK.

SEMPER FIDELIS.
MARCH.

By John Philip Sousa.

THE MARCH PAST of the NATIONAL FENCIBLES.

Tempo di marcia.

By John Philip Sousa.

16   The March Past of the National Fencibles

To
COLUMBIA COMMANDERY No 2
KNIGHTS TEMPLAR
Washington D. C.

THE THUNDERER.
MARCH.

SOUSA.

To Messrs Frank Hatton and Beriah Wilkins.

The Washington Post.

WASHINGTON, SUNDAY, JUNE 16, 1889.—SIXTEEN PAGES.

JOHN F. ELLIS & Co.,
MUSIC PUBLISHERS,
AND DEALERS IN
PIANOS, ORGANS,
AND
MUSICAL INSTRUMENTS,

EDWARD F. DROOP,
Organs,
Æolian Organs,
Sheet Music, Music Books,
Violin Strings and Musical Merchandise of all Descriptions.
NO. 925 PENNSYLVANIA AVENUE.

HENRY EBERBACH,
Dealer in
Pianos, Parlor Organs,
MUSIC, AND
Musical Merchandise,
915 F Street, N. W.

HUGO WORCH AND CO.,
MUSIC PUBLISHERS,
AND IMPORTERS OF
Strings and
Musical Instruments,
SEVENTH ST., N. W.

W. G. Metzerott & Co.,
DEALERS IN
PIANOS, ORGANS,
AND
SHEET MUSIC,
MUSICAL MERCHANDISE
OF ALL DESCRIPTIONS.
1110 F St.—N. W.

Thompsons'Music Store
PIANOS
AND
Musical Merchandise,
Sheet Music, Books, Strings &c.
524 Eleventh St.

HENRY WHITE,
Music Dealer & Publisher,
935 F. St.

Franz Waldecker & Co.,
719 Seventh St. N. W.
SHEET MUSIC,
MUSICAL INSTRUMENTS
AND MERCHANDISE.

G. L. WILD & BROS.,
DEALERS IN
PIANOS, ORGANS,
ORCHESTRONES,
Sheet Music,
Music Books,
and Musical Instruments
of all kinds.
709 SEVENTH ST., N. W.

YOUNG AUTHORS.

Thousands on the
Smithsonian Grounds.

Medals for Essays.

The Winners of The Washington Post's Prizes.

Address by Justice Miller.

ALBAUGH'S
GRAND OPERA HOUSE.

Mr. Albaugh takes great pleasure in announcing a

Grand Concert!
In aid for Fund for the
Johnstown Sufferers!
Sunday Evening, June 16
On which occasion
100 MUSICIANS
—OF—
Washington and Georgetown
Have been combined and organized by
Conductor of Orchestra Mr. R. C. BERNAYS.
SOUSA. Together with the

Lamont Opera Company

March
4
by John Philip Sousa.
DIRECTOR BAND U.S.M.C.

PHILADELPHIA: Published by HARRY COLEMAN.

Copyrighted 1889 by Harry Coleman.

THE WASHINGTON POST.

MARCH.

SOUSA.

Tempo marziale.

THE PICADOR MARCH

BY JOHN PHILIP SOUSA

Director of U.S. Marine Band.

FULL ORCHESTRA $1.00 — BAND 50¢
SMALL ORCHESTRA 60¢ — PIANO 40¢

PHILADELPHIA: Published by HARRY COLEMAN, Nº 228 NORTH 9TH ST.

THE PICADORE MARCH.

SOUSA.

PIANO.

MARCH

THE

HIGH SCHOOL CADETS

FOR PIANO BY

JOHN PHILIP SOUSA

PUBLISHED BY

HARRY COLEMAN

PHILADELPHIA, PA.

THE HIGH SCHOOL CADETS.
MARCH.

SOUSA.

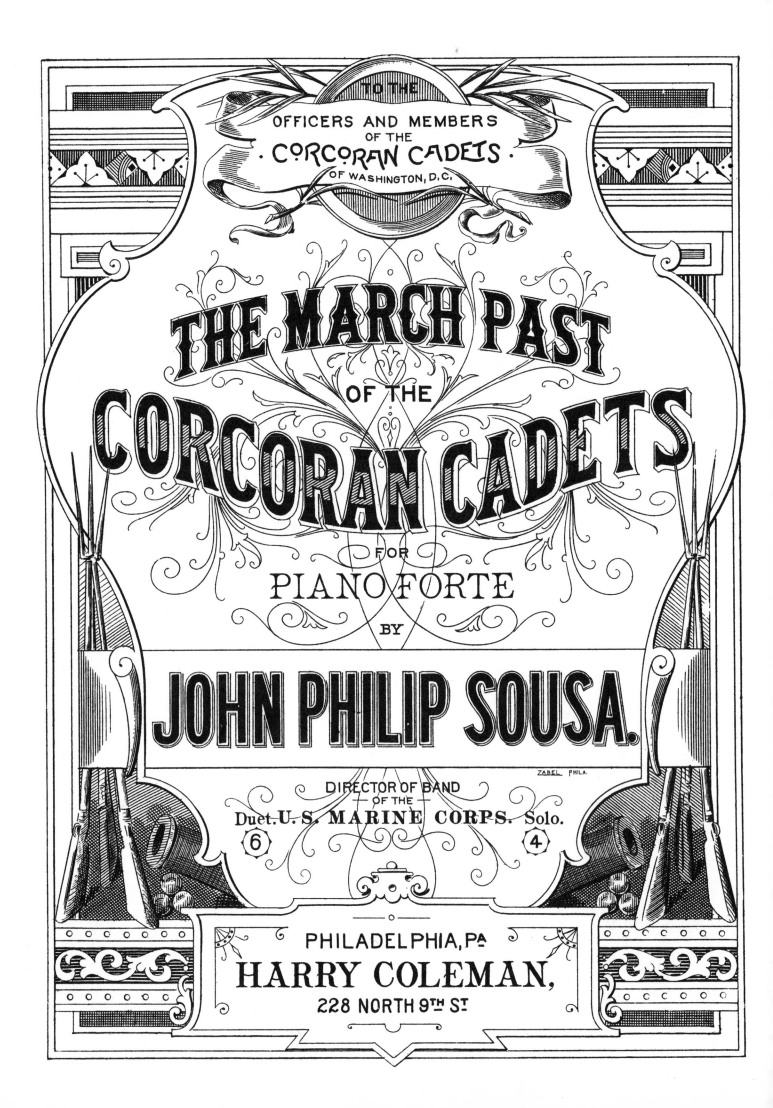

To the Officers and Members
of the
CORCORAN CADETS of Washington D.C.

THE MARCH PAST
OF THE
CORCORAN CADETS.

SOUSA.

Tempo marziale.

with the Corc'- ran swing, On - ward, sol - dier dar - - ing! *ff*

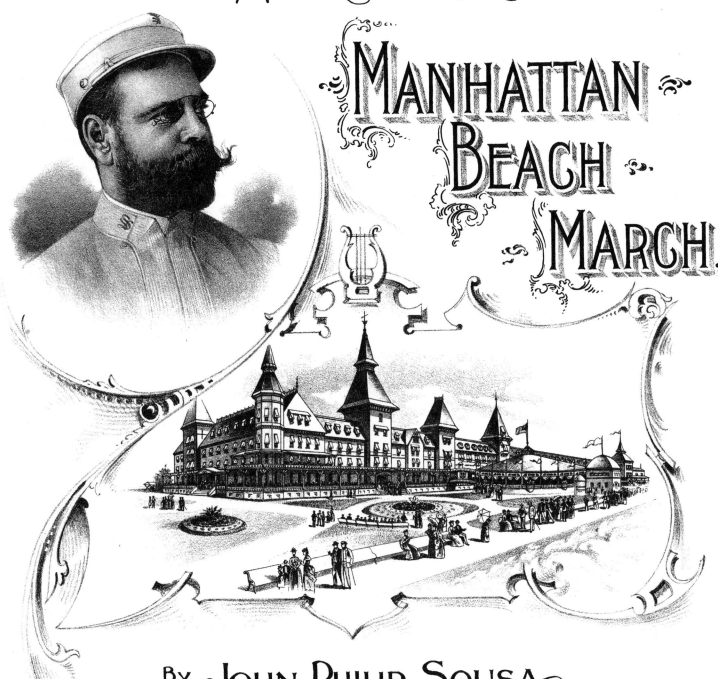

· TO ·
AUSTIN CORBIN, ESQ.

MANHATTAN BEACH MARCH.

BY JOHN PHILIP SOUSA.

PIANO 2 HANDS 50.
PIANO 4 HANDS 1.00
PIANO 6 HANDS 1.50
ORCHESTRA 1.00
MILITARY BAND 50.
ZITHER SOLO 40.

ZITHER DUET 50.
MANDOLIN SOLO 40.
MANDOLIN & PIANO 60.
MANDOLIN & GUITAR 50.
MANDOLIN-PIANO & GUITAR 75.
2 MANDOLINS & PIANO 75.

2 MANDOLINS & GUITAR, 60.
GUITAR SOLO 40.
GUITAR DUET 50.
BANJO SOLO 40.
BANJO DUET 50.
BANJO & PIANO 50.

PUBLISHED BY

THE JOHN CHURCH COMPANY.

CINCINNATI,   NEW YORK,   CHICAGO.

THE MANHATTAN BEACH
MARCH.

JOHN PHILIP SOUSA.

Tempo Marche Militaire.

THE LIBERTY BELL MARCH.

By JOHN PHILIP SOUSA.

PIANO 2 HANDS 50.
PIANO 4 HANDS 1.00
PIANO 6 HANDS 1.50
ORCHESTRA 1.00
MILITARY BAND 50.
GUITAR DUET 50.

ZITHER SOLO 40.
ZITHER DUET 50.
MANDOLIN SOLO 40.
MANDOLIN & PIANO 60.
MANDOLIN & GUITAR 50.

MANDOLIN-PIANO & GUITAR 75.
GUITAR SOLO 40.
BANJO SOLO 40.
BANJO DUET 50.
BANJO & PIANO 50.
2 MANDOLINS & GUITAR, 60.

PUBLISHED BY

THE JOHN CHURCH COMPANY.

CINCINNATI,
NEW YORK,   CHICAGO.

THE LIBERTY BELL
MARCH.

JOHN PHILIP SOUSA.

SOUSA'S FAMOUS MARCHES

AND OTHER COMPOSITIONS FOR PIANOFORTE

Simplified Edition without Octaves for Little Fingers

For Teachers and Pupils

PUBLISHED BY

HARRY COLEMAN.

PHILADELPHIA PA.

THE BEAU IDEAL MARCH.

SOUSA.

Written for
THE COTTON STATES AND INTERNATIONAL EXPOSITION.
ATLANTA, 1895.

KING COTTON MARCH.

BY JOHN PHILIP SOUSA.

PIANO 2 HANDS 50.	2 MANDOLINS & GUITAR, 60.
PIANO 4 HANDS 1.00	GUITAR SOLO 40.
PIANO 6 HANDS 1.50	GUITAR DUET 50.
ORCHESTRA 1.00	BANJO SOLO 40.
MILITARY BAND 50.	BANJO DUET 50.
ZITHER SOLO 40.	BANJO & PIANO 50.

ZITHER DUET 50.
MANDOLIN SOLO 40.
MANDOLIN & PIANO 60.
MANDOLIN & GUITAR 50.
MANDOLIN-PIANO & GUITAR 75.
2 MANDOLINS & PIANO 75.

PUBLISHED BY

THE JOHN CHURCH COMPANY.

CINCINNATI,   NEW YORK,   CHICAGO.

KING COTTON

MARCH.

John Philip Sousa.

EL CAPITAN MARCH.

BY JOHN PHILIP SOUSA.

PIANO 2 HANDS 50.
PIANO 4 HANDS 1.00
PIANO 6 HANDS 1.50
ORCHESTRA 1.00
MILITARY BAND 50.
ZITHER SOLO 40.

ZITHER DUET 50.
MANDOLIN SOLO 40.
MANDOLIN & PIANO 60.
MANDOLIN & GUITAR 50.
MANDOLIN-PIANO & GUITAR 75.
2 MANDOLINS & PIANO 75.

2 MANDOLINS & GUITAR, 60.
GUITAR SOLO 40.
GUITAR DUET 50.
BANJO SOLO 40.
BANJO DUET 50.
BANJO & PIANO 50.

PUBLISHED BY

THE JOHN CHURCH COMPANY.

CINCINNATI,   NEW YORK,   CHICAGO.

EL CAPITAN.

MARCH.

JOHN PHILIP SOUSA.

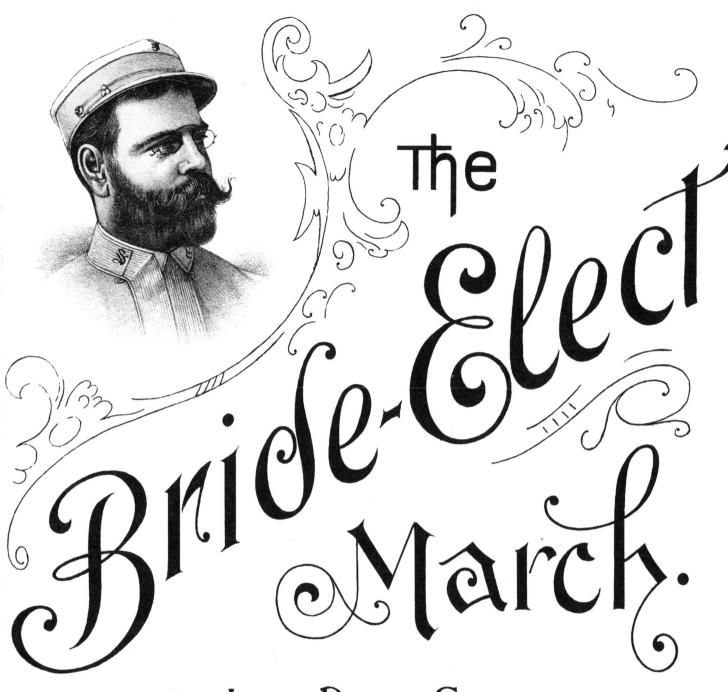

The Bride-Elect March.

By John Philip Sousa.

Piano 2 Hands 50.		2 Mandolins & Guitar, 70.
Piano 4 Hands 1.00		Guitar Solo 40.
Piano 6 Hands 1.50	Zither Duet 90.	Guitar Duet 50.
Orchestra 1.00	Mandolin Solo 40.	Banjo Solo 40.
Military Band 50.	Mandolin & Piano 60.	Banjo Duet 50.
Zither Solo 50.	Mandolin & Guitar 50.	Banjo & Piano 60.
	Mandolin-Piano & Guitar 80.	
	2 Mandolins & Piano 80.	

PUBLISHED BY

The John Church Company.

CINCINNATI, NEW YORK, CHICAGO, LEIPSIC.

The Bride-Elect

MARCH.

JOHN PHILIP SOUSA.

THE STARS AND STRIPES FOREVER! MARCH.

By John Philip Sousa.

PIANO 2 HANDS 50.
PIANO 4 HANDS 1.00
PIANO 6 HANDS 1.50
ORCHESTRA 1.00
MILITARY BAND 50.
ZITHER SOLO 50.

ZITHER DUET 90.
MANDOLIN SOLO 40.
MANDOLIN & PIANO 60.
MANDOLIN & GUITAR 50.
MANDOLIN-PIANO & GUITAR 80.
2 MANDOLINS & PIANO 80.

2 MANDOLINS & GUITAR, 70.
GUITAR SOLO 40.
GUITAR DUET 50.
BANJO SOLO 40.
BANJO DUET 50.
BANJO & PIANO 60.

PUBLISHED BY

THE JOHN CHURCH COMPANY.

CINCINNATI,   NEW YORK,   CHICAGO,   LEIPSIC.

The Stars and Stripes Forever.

March.

JOHN PHILIP SOUSA.

STARS AND STRIPES FOREVER! SONG.

BY JOHN PHILIP SOUSA.

PUBLISHED BY

THE JOHN CHURCH COMPANY.

CINCINNATI, NEW YORK, CHICAGO, LEIPSIC.

The Stars and Stripes Forever.

SONG.

Words and Music by

JOHN PHILIP SOUSA.

Tempo di Marcia.

1. Let
2. Let

mar - tial note   In   tri - umph float, And   lib - er - ty   ex - tend   its
ea - gle shriek   From   lof - ty peak, The   nev - er - end - ing watch-word

might - y   hand,   A   flag   ap - pears,   'Mid   thun - d'rous cheers,   The
of   our   land.   Let   sum - mer breeze   Waft   through   the   trees   The

na - tions may deem their flags the best And__ cheer them with fer - vid e-

la - tion, But the flag of the North and South and West Is the

flag of flags, The flag of Free-dom's na - - tion. Hur - rah for the flag of the

CHORUS.

free,_____ May it wave as our stand - ard for - ev - - - er, The

The Stars and Stripes Forever (song)

"*A sudden thought strikes me,—*
Let us swear an eternal friendship."

MARCH
Hands across the Sea.

BY JOHN PHILIP SOUSA.

PIANO 2 HANDS 50.
PIANO 4 HANDS 1.00
PIANO 6 HANDS 1.50
ORCHESTRA 1.00
MILITARY BAND 50.
ZITHER SOLO 50.

ZITHER DUET 90.
MANDOLIN SOLO 40.
MANDOLIN & PIANO 60.
MANDOLIN & GUITAR 50.
MANDOLIN-PIANO & GUITAR 80.
2 MANDOLINS & PIANO 80.

2 MANDOLINS & GUITAR, 70.
GUITAR SOLO 40.
GUITAR DUET 50.
BANJO SOLO 40.
BANJO DUET 50.
BANJO & PIANO 60.

PUBLISHED BY

THE JOHN CHURCH COMPANY.

CINCINNATI, NEW YORK, CHICAGO, LEIPSIC.

Hands across the Sea.

MARCH.

JOHN PHILIP SOUSA.

Tempo di marcia.

HAIL TO
THE SPIRIT OF LIBERTY
MARCH

BY JOHN PHILIP SOUSA.

COMPOSED EXPRESSLY FOR,
AND PLAYED FOR THE FIRST TIME
AT THE DEDICATION OF THE~
LA FAYETTE · MONUMENT
IN PARIS,
JULY 4TH 1900.

Piano 2 Hands....50.
Piano 4 Hands........1.00
Piano 6 Hands..........1.50
Orchestra................1.00
Military Band......50.
Zither Solo....50.

2 Mandolins & Guitar.........70.
Guitar Solo..................40.
Guitar Duet................50.
Banjo Solo.............40.
Banjo Duet.........50.
Banjo & Piano.....60.

Zither Duet......90.
Mandolin Solo..........40.
Mandolin & Piano......60.
Mandolin & Guitar......50.
Mandolin, Piano & Guitar....80.
2 Mandolins & Piano...80.

·THE·
JOHN CHURCH COMPANY,
Cincinnati, Chicago, New York,
Leipsic, London.

Hail to
The Spirit of Liberty
MARCH.

JOHN PHILIP SOUSA.

The Invincible Eagle March

By John Philip Sousa.

Piano 2 Hands 50.
Piano 4 Hands 1.00
Piano 6 Hands 1.50
Orchestra 1.00
Military Band 50.
Zither Solo 40.

Zither Duet 50.
Mandolin Solo 40.
Mandolin & Piano 60.
Mandolin & Guitar 50.
Mandolin-Piano & Guitar 75.
2 Mandolins & Piano 75.

2 Mandolins & Guitar, 60.
Guitar Solo 40.
Guitar Duet 50.
Banjo Solo 40.
Banjo Duet 50.
Banjo & Piano 50.

The John Church Company.

CINCINNATI, CHICAGO, NEW YORK, LEIPSIC, LONDON.

The Invincible Eagle.

MARCH.

JOHN PHILIP SOUSA.

90   The Invincible Eagle

RESPECTFULLY DEDICATED
BY SPECIAL PERMISSION TO HIS MOST GRACIOUS MAJESTY
EDWARD VII.

Military March

Imperial Edward

BY
JOHN PHILIP SOUSA.

PIANO 2 HANDS .50
PIANO 4 HANDS 1⁰⁰
PIANO 6 HANDS 1⁵⁰
ORCHESTRA 1⁰⁰
MILITARY BAND .50
ZITHER SOLO .40

ZITHER DUET .70
MANDOLIN SOLO .40
MANDOLIN & PIANO .60
MANDOLIN & GUITAR .50
MANDOLIN-PIANO & GUITAR .80
2 MANDOLINS & PIANO .80

2 MANDOLINS & GUITAR .70
GUITAR SOLO .40
GUITAR DUET .50
BANJO SOLO .40
BANJO DUET .50
BANJO & PIANO .60

PUBLISHED BY
THE JOHN CHURCH COMPANY
CINCINNATI, CHICAGO, NEW YORK, LEIPSIC, LONDON.

Imperial Edward, Military March.

John Philip Sousa

JACK TAR MARCH.

BY JOHN PHILIP SOUSA.

PIANO 2 HANDS 50.	MANDOLIN SOLO 40.	GUITAR SOLO 40.
PIANO 4 HANDS 1.00	MANDOLIN & PIANO 60.	GUITAR DUET 50.
ORCHESTRA 1.00	MANDOLIN & GUITAR 50.	BANJO SOLO 40.
MILITARY BAND 50.	MANDOLIN-PIANO & GUITAR 80.	BANJO DUET 50.
	2 MANDOLINS & PIANO 80.	BANJO & PIANO 60.
	2 MANDOLINS & GUITAR, 70.	

PUBLISHED BY

THE JOHN CHURCH COMPANY.

CINCINNATI, NEW YORK, CHICAGO,

LEIPSIC, LONDON.

Jack Tar.
March.

JOHN PHILIP SOUSA.

(Sailor's Hornpipe.)

THE DIPLOMAT

MARCH.

BY JOHN PHILIP SOUSA.

PIANO 2 HANDS 50.	MANDOLIN SOLO 40.	GUITAR SOLO 40.
PIANO 4 HANDS 1.00	MANDOLIN & PIANO 60.	GUITAR DUET 50.
ORCHESTRA 1.00	MANDOLIN & GUITAR 50.	BANJO SOLO 40.
MILITARY BAND 50.	MANDOLIN-PIANO & GUITAR 80.	BANJO DUET 50.
	2 MANDOLINS & PIANO 80.	BANJO & PIANO 60.
	2 MANDOLINS & GUITAR, 70.	

PUBLISHED BY

THE JOHN CHURCH COMPANY.

CINCINNATI, NEW YORK, CHICAGO,

LEIPSIC, LONDON.

The Diplomat.
March.

JOHN PHILIP SOUSA.

106   The Diplomat

THE FREE LANCE MARCH.

BY JOHN PHILIP SOUSA.

PIANO 2 HANDS 50.
PIANO 4 HANDS 1.00
PIANO 6 HANDS 1.50
ORCHESTRA 1.00
MILITARY BAND 50.
ZITHER SOLO 50.

ZITHER DUET 50.
MANDOLIN SOLO 40.
MANDOLIN & PIANO 60.
MANDOLIN & GUITAR 50.
MANDOLIN-PIANO & GUITAR 75.
2 MANDOLINS & PIANO 75.

2 MANDOLINS & GUITAR, 60.
GUITAR SOLO 40.
GUITAR DUET 50.
BANJO SOLO 40.
BANJO DUET 50.
BANJO & PIANO 50.

PUBLISHED BY

THE JOHN CHURCH COMPANY.

CINCINNATI,   NEW YORK,   CHICAGO,

LEIPSIC,   LONDON.

The Free Lance.
March.

JOHN PHILIP SOUSA.

Marcia Spiritoso.